ACROSS COBBLE-STONES

ACROSS COBBLE-STONES

by
DERRICK V. RUGG

Drawings by
CLAIRE WESTERN

TABB HOUSE
Padstow, Cornwall.

First published 1983
Tabb House, 11 Church Street, Padstow, Cornwall PL28 8BG

I WOULD LIKE to express my gratitude for the loan of photographs, to Mrs S. G. Blackmore, Mrs J. Bowles, Mrs P. Chave, Mrs W. S. Gibbins, Mrs F. Goff, Mr Leslie Leatt, Mrs Tom Manfield, Mrs D. A. Muchamore, Mr Clifford Pike, Mr Owen Rugg, Mr Bert Selway, Mrs D. Sprague, and Mrs F. Western. I am grateful to Mrs Claire Western for making the drawings on the cover and in the book, and thanks are also due to the Reverend Jack Goodall for help and advice.

Printed in Great Britain by Quintrell & Co. Ltd., Wadebridge, Cornwall.
Bound by R. Booth (Bookbinders) Ltd, Carnstead, Mabe, Cornwall.

Contents

List of Illustrations

PHOTOGRAPHS

DRAWINGS of Kentisbeare,
by Claire Western

CHAPTER 1

Early Days

I HAVE a mind to write of days that have gone — some well remembered and others remembered to have been remembered. I begin with an afternoon in the early thirties. There was an anguished crying. A pram rocked with the yearning for the feel of a hand, or the sight of a smiling face in the hoods opening on to a lonely, blue void. Can you comprehend that shaded aloneness on a summer day? A face came and with it, silence. The face went and draining tears came burning back. . . oblivion. I have such a memory still. I know where the pram must have been: away from the back door of Silver Park in Kentisbeare, for it always was put there by Mother. "Down by the logs", we called it.

Mother had plenty to do, with the home, a baby that followed me after fourteen months, and quite a few hens to look after. I have been told I was jealous of my brother Dennis, having attacked him, even with a hammer.

"Watch that boy or he will kill the little one!" Gran Rugg said, and I was sent across to her a lot, until each particularly violent mood subsided. Thus, I became a favourite with that Gran, so that on every possible occasion she *procured* (borrowed) me, until Mother grew annoyed about it. Gran possessed endless patience, a lively humour, and plenty of boy psychology.

She had a large tin containing a great variety of buttons, with quite a few of the brass, military kind, besides little oval-shaped mustard tins full of farthings, all in the dark recesses of a corner cupboard. If anyone grew tired of sorting into sets (before modern Maths was heard of), then there was a piece of sandpaper handy to polish the steel strip of the fender.

Another activity was folding and cutting newspaper into 'squibs' to light pipes or oil lamps, at the grate. These were pushed into an earthenware pot, which seemed to possess an infinite capacity.

In spite of Mother's remonstrations, I was allowed to chop sticks on the old elm block that had come from the tree that once stood by the village pound.

Gran had Beauty of Bath apples on the spare bedroom floor, up to Christmas, and an old lady left pear-drops for some reason, for somebody. I ate them.

There was, however, in that thatched house of cob a dimension I cannot transmit, a presence — or absence. Grandfather, whom I did not remember, was dead, and Mother said, upon my query, that anyone did not ought to say anything about it. Well, he was dead. Yet there was the small medicine glass he had used and the broad beans and kidney beans he had hoarded in a cream-and-black tin. There was a good number of Afrikander tobacco tins decorated with covered wagons, in the table drawer, and Grandfather's Sunday cane brought back from India was hung along a picture of Wimbledon. The front door was never locked so that Grandfather, or Daddy Dido as Gran called him, could come in anytime he wished.

That part was eerie. But somehow it was more than that.

MY BROTHER Dennis survived, after all, though I was a complete autocrat. This resulted in daily fights right up to our teens when we began knocking spots off each other, and the running battle ceased, by unspoken mutual accord.

It was pleasant to sit on the logs on sunny pre-school days and look at the meadows rolling across the valley to the uplands of Ford Farm where Father worked, mainly with the poultry. The farmhouse was down behind the hill, and somewhere over there were the fowls, and all our gazing across the Ken valley we knew would not reveal Father. So we dug with spades to while away the time and measured ourselves against the elms across the field. We seemed as tall as they were as we stood up and shouted for the echoes.

In the distance, about half a mile away, we often saw Bobby Sparkes, one of Father's workmates, working with his team of horses. A cheerful man, badly crippled from a fall out of his pram, he had all the determination there was. I noticed later that when he walked, his firkin of cider nearly touched the ground as he threw himself from side to side.

How many thus disabled would work at all today, let alone follow the plough's trail. . .? But I digress.

Across there in Stony Field or Nodbeare was Bobby, and as he came to the headlands, he would say "Whoa!" in his normal voice, and the wind would carry that and other commands to us. Why, then, should we not shout,"Hello, Hello! Bobby, Bobby!" . . .? If his ordinary voice could carry across the valley over the chimneys of Westhayes to us, then our hollering and waving should attract his attention. He never seemed to hear, though.

"Tell Bobby we shout and wave!" we instructed Father. But through all the days of great vocal exertion, when the seagulls followed Bobby and you could hear their cries mingle with the quiet commands of a man who struggled along as happy as the larks above him, our cries were devoured by the hungry valley.

The same happened at hoeing time, when Father said Harry and Bobby had their summer holidays. The idea was to finish any jobs around the farmstead and get out into the fields as quickly as possible lest the plants grew away from the task force.

"Harry was taking a bit too long with the milking one morning and Farmer Chave wanted to hustle him a bit," Father told me.

"Come on then, Harry! Hat, coat, stick!" the boss is reputed to have said as he assisted the launching. He seemed to have forgotten the firkin, but I am sure Harry, better known as Teeny, didn't.

Punctuating our idling around at the back of the house, horses clip-clopped along the road in front, and sometimes a carter would throw a turnip or swede over the corner of the hedge. That would be one of Father's mates, and they frequently did it for one another.

"Go up and see if there is a swede!" Mother would say. It was like Elijah's barrel of meal, I thought, when I came across the Bible story.

Also, we had a fair number of visitors. There was Sid, the butcher's boy, and Baker James, who always seemed to be in a surly mood.

"His bread is very pudden'y" Mother said to another lady.

"Mother doesn't like your pudden'y bread, Baker!" I said to him when he came that afternoon. The surprised baker banged a loaf down hard enough to crack the scullery table and slammed his way out. I had to go through the mill for my cheek. Well, I had thought I was doing the right thing!

Everything went all right with Mr Warren though. He used to talk and play with us for quite a while on some days, and we used to like to see Eastmond's van from Tiverton pull up. As Mr Warren left, he would sometimes pick up Dennis and say, "Shall I take him?"

"Yes, you can have him!" I would answer.

Then he would pick me up and make to carry me off through the gate. At that, Dennis would scream and bawl like hell. After the way I bossed him around!

FATHER AND I sometimes went across to Gran's house, when I preferred to foot it in spite of the saying about third-class riding being superior to first-class walking. I didn't like riding on the handlebars of a large-ish bicycle, even though the distance was only a couple hundred yards or so. As we freewheeled down the slight incline by Catford Court, with the brake having to be applied because of humans, animals, or traffic, I used to feel sure I would somersault over the front wheel. And I was terrified, too, that my fingers would get mixed up with the brake levers.

Walking suited me fine, especially after dark, when in the light from windows, parish lantern (the moon), or sparse street lamps, the road glistened and there were interesting shadows.

Friday was a day which held a sort of ritual. Gran, who had been in private service for thirty odd years, and who could cook anything without any cook-books, would lay on a special meal for Father, who would then go up to the Wyndham Arms where he sometimes stayed for a long while. I would sit on a low Victorian chair and grow sleepy.

"The dust-man", or was it dusk man? "is coming," Gran would say, and as I watched the pendulum criss-cross behind the window of the mantel clock, I usually fell asleep. But sometimes

I was not asleep when Gran went across to the little window that looked up to the village. She would ease the curtain back and look 'up to the top'.

Many chaps used to have a regular night every week, Friday or Saturday seeming often to be chosen. Then, armed with lanterns, they sallied off and enjoyed themselves. When Paddy, the landlord, kicked them out, they lit their lanterns and went home. Well, not always!

"That's so and so," Gran would say to herself, and me. "Here comes Jack Salisbury. Down he goes!" Then she would laugh like the blazes, and relay any further gymnastics of that swain or his fellows.

Eventually I arrived home, when Mother often carried on about me being too late. I don't remember Dennis going with me on those occasions, but I had stayed with Gran at Dennis's arrival and she hadn't wanted to give me up. She had even bought a pushchair, and I was pushed around, whenever I could be procured, right up to the time of starting school. I was all too obviously the favourite, and Mother sometimes carried on about that, too.

Kentisbeare

But Dennis *did* come along to Guddiford Mills where we had another grandmother and grandfather. We didn't seem to go very often, and Father was always missing as far as I can remember, on account of it being somewhat cool between him and Grandfer.

When we did visit, we sat in the settle and never stirred.

"I will say one thing," remarked Gran Goff to Mother. "Your boys are well behaved. They don't say a word."

Perhaps reader — if you are still with me — you think we were 'kept down'. No, that was not it at all. As we sat in the settle, we were too busy listening to the conversation to do anything else.

It was quite likely that a neighbour or two would be there particularly at haytime or harvest, and certainly Uncle Arthur, Jack Salisbury, and perhaps Aunt Evelyn and Uncle Bert.

Grandfather always made his own cider and would bring it in from the cellar in the mill. Then he would pour it out from one of those floral jugs with peculiar handles, into mugs.

"Give the boys half a tea-cup!" he would instruct, and we had our ration in frail china cups with blue flowers on them that everyone seemed to have in those days.

The talk would be lively, while an abrupt thin note would join in at intervals. I used to feel muzzy with the cider, and I would look around the room to discover where the interruption came from. The terse utterance just didn't match up with the great brass-faced clock in the corner.

Uncle Arthur would 'talk like a dutch uncle' when he had had quite a small amount of cider, and if Grandfer could be induced to play the tin whistle, Uncle would put on a sailor's hat he had from the 1914-18 war and dance around with Dennis or any small child available, in a rather ludicrous way, I suppose. Dipping the mouthpiece of his tin whistle in his cider, Grandfer would play about Antonio and his ice-cream cart, and 'Felix Keeps on Walking', 'Show me the Way to go Home' and 'The Sets', as he termed The Lancers.

Sometimes people danced, seriously I mean, and then Grandfer's frowning in respect of Uncle Arthur subsided and he seemed to smile, if that is possible behind a tin whistle.

Eventually, the music would stop and the evening's entertainment was over.

"Ev'ee got a kiss for Gran!"

Then it was happily-wearily home.

I BEGAN to think about school; and when the two Tidball girls from next door came in, they told of doing sums, of writing and reading, etc. They also mentioned the teachers: Mrs Spratt, Mr Painter-or Archie and Mrs Painter. The last-named lady was fierce, they said. "Er gets as red as a turkey cock!" somebody warned. With such snippets coming pretty regularly, I began to wonder what the Infant Room would be like, and I began to make pictures in my mind. I visualised a long table with a lot of boys and girls along it in tea-party fashion. I was way off target, as it turned out.

But I was too young to go to school, and I had, along with Dennis, to do 'pretend' sums and scribble 'wavy-line' letters for the Tidball girls to post to Father Christmas.

"You do post them, Florrie?"

"Yes," she said, "of course I posts 'em."

There was the shopping to do, which reduced the tedium; and that entailed writing out a list and standing on the pedals of an old bicycle that was propped against the wall. After perhaps an hour of sitting on the machine and getting off and moving it at intervals, first outwards and then back, the invisible groceries arrived home for Mother to check. She always managed to find time to enter into the spirit of things.

"What is he up to?" people asked.

"Oh, he is getting the shopping," Mother said. "He is a very good boy at that."

Father brought home tins, mainly from a dump near his work, and I remember building them up, transferring covers and what not. Apparently, I covered any open receptacle in the house — including the chamber pots.

Occasionally, Dennis and I would rush out to the gate. A threshing tackle would be coming up the road. It was likely to belong to the Manfield Brothers, and we would shout and wave at the two smutty men on the great 'steamer', and watch as the threshing drum passed along, followed by the straw tier with a couple of bicycles dangling from it. Of course, we wanted to be engine drivers when we grew up, and we admired the procession — having no idea of the torture it carried to the farm labourer, sweating amid the dust from sheaves, at the mercy of a machine that never tired and seldom broke down.

Sometimes a beautiful 'female' traction came steaming along. It was called the Queen Mary and it belonged to Jimmy Vinnicombe. Jimmy only had one tackle — like Little Claus with his horse — and he must have been tremendously proud of his steam engine, for its brown and gold was polished to an apposite regality.

Another event that brought a change and a stir was the arrival of the bazaar, in the shape of a large van hung all over with baskets, buckets, and pans. I was absolutely fascinated by the skilful usage of all the hanging space, and I remember that the man who drove the vehicle seemed to regard everyone as a potential bazaar-lifter.

But I so wanted to go to school! In the meantime, I had to make do with fighting Dennis and looking forward to Mr Warren, and Mr West of Trump's Stores in Ottery.

Mr West was a smallish, smiling man who wore horn-rimmed spectacles and had glossy, curly, brown hair that *had* to be noticed. He came in, sat down, and opened a bag that he always carried. All the children in the houses he visited received broken biscuits, along with a bit of good-natured chaffing.

Mr West took the orders and later in the week a larger van pulled up with the groceries.

"Run and get the groceries," Mother would say and Dennis and I would run to collect a box at the tail of the van from a man whose smile substituted for words. Jesse Baker was no doubt anticipating a pint of cider at the Wyndham Arms.

Someone from Newton Poppleford came to collect eggs, and Mr Rice called. Ricie was a greengrocer from Exeter. He had a lorry with sliding doors to keep the cats from the fish and, I daresay, boys from oranges and bananas.

When he arrived, he 'called'! He made loud, weird noises that I used to try and make sense of, and if no-one came out, he

Silver Street. Gran Rugg's cottage on the corner

Harry Lane

Derrick & Dennis Rugg

Guddiford Mill

Uncle Edward

pushed his shiny red face over the gate.

"I don't think I want anything today," Mother would quite often say. Ricie explained that he had this, that, and the other, and so usually sold something. Of course, I hoped it was a banana, if only an over-ripe cheap one.

The quick-tongued, cheerful trader seemed to supply everybody with orange boxes, for hens to lay in.

Ricie hurried along – also anticipating refreshment at the Wyndham Arms.

CHAPTER 2

School – At Last

THE DAY at last dawned when I found myself on my way to school, and I can bring back clearly the events of that early morning.

The Tidball children came excitedly in from next door. I was their protegé, their responsibility to take and return from school. Mothers didn't fill that role for the most part in those days – and it was not such a bad omission, I feel, as children are often drawn to tears as the whistle goes and Mum has to leave.

There seemed to be a deeply-touching possessiveness about taking a new recruit to school, and I can see now the faces of little children, barely older than their charges, flushed with pride in their responsibility. In that way, I set out in 1934, hand in hand with vying sponsors, all of us stretched right across the road to school. A quarter of a mile further on the chain was broken, and we joined an assembly of young folk about the chestnut tree in Kentisbeare village.

Older boys in hobnailed boots, giants to me, stamped around and inspected all newcomers, enquiring names and pedigrees, making remarks, joking, and boasting of their disrespect for teachers. When we filtered down to the playground, the tours of inspection continued, and one large farmer's boy, Francis Blackmore, discovered that I had a penny.

"You can spend 'ee at Bessie Rowe's," he said. "Get on!"

After receiving directions, I went back up Fore Street hill and duly passed the smithy. Then I tried a door. It was shut.

"It never is!" insisted Francis, when I reported back. "The door is always open."

The school bell, I suppose, must have been imminent because Franny, as they called him, grew very agitated, and was no doubt torn between becoming late for school and ensuring that my penny was spent. Suddenly he grabbed hold of me, and I was spending my princely sum of money in Bessie's shop before you could say Jack Robinson. I can't remember what I bought, but liquorice pipes, chewing gum, gobstoppers, sherbet, chocolate tobacco and suchlike were available.

The bell rang and the peculiar medley of the playground died away. We were placed in lines from which we filtered into the Infant Room.

I looked for the long, social tables. But where were they? Instead, there were little brown affairs at which two children sat on small straight-backed chairs, and I was soon put alongside another boy.

I was puzzled and fascinated by the large-ish, high room. The lower border was painted in a dark, glossy colour, and all above was yellow. Quaint ventilators were spaced around the heights, and chandeliers hung from chains. I recall one picture of a boy and girl picking primroses and another showing a great-crested

Bessie Rowe's emporium

grebe on its nest. A bead frame was conspicuous along with a green cupboard with square doors, and up front was a guarded fireplace and a great galvanised fire bucket. And, oh yes, there was a teacher — Mrs Spratt. She was very old, I thought, round-faced and rather ruddy in complexion. Dark, long black dresses were the firm rule with Mrs Spratt, I found, and beads and ear-rings were always worn. A comb was carefully positioned at the back of the head to fix an unchanging hairstyle, and every time Teacher turned, my eyes were somehow drawn to the precision of it all.

Such a miscellany of things I remember. But there were lessons too, of course. Mrs Spratt was an essentially warm-hearted old soul who had taught our mothers and fathers before us. But if the truth be told, she was getting a bit past it. Some of the boys would play her up or evoke frustration by their wooden-headed stupidity, and she would on occasions successfully drag them off to the Head. Quite often, though, a boy would stick his heels against table legs and resist so effectively that the operation had to be abandoned. Harold Leatt was good at that.

A short, brown cane was used frequently and without much force: therefore, it carried no disciplinary weight, most of us collecting our regular swipe with nonchalance.

When Teacher moved around the room, some of the braves would walk around behind her, manoeuvring so as always to be in that position. I never plucked up enough courage for this, but was convulsed at some of the antics, especially at Lovis Lane, who did the following act with the added refinement of walking half out of Wellington boots. Mrs Spratt did not seem to be aware of her retinue of comics.

But I seem to remember I mentioned lessons. I will start with reading, though I don't really know which aspect I ought to give priority. There was a grubby Beacon Reader which one read page by page, anyone being strictly forbidden to look ahead. I recall our stories: 'Little Red Hen', 'The Hobyars', 'Careful Hans', and a good many others.

Then there was daily alphabetic practice: c-a-t, cat; m-a-t, mat, etc., which involved a chart or blackboard, a pointer — and of course, Mrs Spratt. I am convinved that the pincer movement didn't catch many readers, and it was a good job some of us were able to teach ourselves.

I will expand this by recording that once I had picked up a few words, I noted how parts of those words appeared in others, and through commonsense and context clues, I worked out new words. The formula was self advancing and you could say that a good many of us learned to read like that in spite of Teacher. I fully appreciate now the extent to which the less able were lambasted with useless alphabetic drill; a starvation diet of a page a day, without visual aids or supporting materials. It must have been hellish; with the chance of learning to read on that basis, slim indeed.

Luckily for the strugglers, and unluckily for their 'tutors', young folk who had cottoned on to words were awarded a pupil to help along each day. My pupil was especially slow-witted, and I know I dug him on the ribs many times, when he would shake and sob. It still cuts me when I think of my prodding and taunting, but the job of getting one's less bright pals off the ground in reading was frustrating in the extreme. Nevertheless, that's largely how it started and I ought to explain that most of the tutors were more considerate and patient than I.

Sums were a different tale as far as I was concerned. Tables were all right, for they just seemed to click into my head in double-quick time, but subtraction presented a problem. When confronted with a situation where the bottom figure was bigger than the top figure, you had to borrow and then do the moral thing; pay back. Perhaps I had been absent when the working had been demonstrated on the board, but I know I just didn't get the message. I tried guessing the figures in my answers, thinking that I must sometimes hit on the right one. Of course, I never did, and teacher, who simply couldn't understand what I was up to, kept sending me over to an abacus, which was then known as a bead frame. There, not knowing what I was supposed to see or do, I cried during quite a few sessions before morning play.

Then one day I saw the light, and my discomfiture fell abruptly away.

"HOW ARE YOU getting on at school?" Mother would ask.

"All right," I used to answer.

"Whom do you play with?" was the inevitable follow-up, which I soon learned to anticipate. I used to sigh, being inwardly very sore at the repetition.

"I don't play with anyone!"

"Why don't you? Couldn't you play with he or she, or so-and-so?"

And so it went on to my increasing annoyance, for I realised Mother thought I didn't have any friends and must therefore be unhappy. I tried to explain that I was as happy as a lark, for so I was. But it didn't seem to sink in.

When I arrived at school in the morning, I used to stand at the edge of the playground that served the big girls and the Infants, and I used to watch the older girls skipping and playing to the accompaniments of ditties like 'Nuts in May', 'Lucy Locket lost her Pocket' and 'Granny's Footsteps'. I used also to watch the bigger boys rolling their hoops, wheels, and tyres into the school premises, and there was quite enough to look at to thoroughly strain the interest and curiosity. At playtime, I carried on the role of spectator, wandering around the gravelly play area, watching the sun freckle on the brick walls – watching everything there was to watch, in fact.

But there was also something special to watch, something I looked for, immediately playtime started. I was; no, I must not give the name.

There was a dark-haired, pretty, farmer's daughter, who used often to stand by her sister. I grew to regard her constantly. I can see her now, hopping from foot to foot, dressed in a blue woollen frock with a pattern of holes. I was no more than adequately turned out, and she seemed so neat and fresh and altogether sweet. I was the tin soldier and she was my dancer to gaze at all the time. She, that girl in blue, was a class above me, but there was an indescribable pleasure in just holding her in view. I blew kisses sometimes when her face was turned slightly away.

So I was happy, and even when I joined in playing horses to Mother's great relief, I still had one eye on the princess, just a couple of years distant in age, but a couple of miles in station from me.

As the years went by I remained silently constant, and after school would follow with feigned nonchalance at a respectful distance. Then a day came when I was dreaming home, on my own as I thought, when a voice said, "Your collar is up, Derrick."

At the same moment, two hands came up and put the matter right. I was overcome with confusion and inexplicable feelings. My existence was realised. My name, too, was known! In that most magic of moments, my heart wanted to melt away, and silent adoration was sweetened and sustained.

Thus enchanted, anyone could put up with the dreary, chanting routines of Mrs Spratt's classroom, and I do not have memories of boredom, for I was introverted, and could entertain myself through my eyes and thoughts. I soon got the hang of printing, where you had to put balls on sticks; an o was a ball, a b was a ball and a stick, etc., and I began to write little stories that were shown to the Head. In scripture, we began with the Garden of Eden, and as the great stories of the Old Testament were recounted, I grew more and more gripped by them.

But Oxo tins half full of plasticine drew forth no creative quality. I used to roll and roll, and then prop up the cover of the tin on four flabby columns. It was about the same with knitting coarse wool on thick, wooden needles. Mrs Spratt used to talk of putting in the ferret, laying the net ready, and then catching a rabbit, but it didn't add up to any knitting, or rabbits, for me. With raffia and milk tops I was inexpert, and the few boxes of coloured wooden shapes were given to the ones who were habitually restless; as I was a comparatively 'good boy', I was missed out. I felt aggrieved about this for the moment, but I was never unhappy for any length of time.

I enjoyed a good part of the work and I could sit and dream away any cloying time. And at playtime, of course, there was always the allure of a little maiden in blue.

ON ARRIVING in the village square at morning, there were several options. If anyone had any money, the choice was quite likely to be Bessie Rowe's tiny sweet-and-tobacco shop half way up High Street hill, where a sizeable group lingered, studying the contents of numerous boxes put on to the counter by Bessie, or Bill, who was an amiable cripple. You could say that Bessie aimed at the lower end of the market, stocking where cheapness and long-lasting properties came together. 'Chews' and various liquorice shapes were popular buys, and so were cardboard cylinders out of which you were supposed to suck sherbet through a liquorice tube, but which you usually up-ended to shake the contents into your palm.

There were three other shops: Miller's Supply Stores, the Post Office, and opposite the school a little shop that was part of Baker James' emporium. That shop was managed by the baker's housekeeper and what she made out of it would be classed today as perks. Well, I have often wondered how much the popular elderly lady made out of her chocolate drops. For a penny you received a triangular bagful of sweets, which was held by the two top corners and whizzed over and over to secure it. I don't recall any weighing. I have sat all morning in the Infant Room surreptitiously eating chocolate drops. I reckon Kentisbeare school-children got Miss Authers' perks.

The quiet old lady died whilst I was in the Infants and a lot of the older children went to her funeral.

If, as was likely, you hadn't a halfpenny, let alone a penny, you could wander into the playground and play. But you could also tease Charlie Lane, the man who cleaned the school, lit the fires, and so on. Charlie was a lively middle-aged card who earned his living several ways. He cut the churchyard — and hair — and said, "Amen" during church services, when he gathered potentially 'difficult' boys into his pew. He passed a sweet along to all the occupants half-way through proceedings, and we reckoned he sucked away himself to cover up the cider he regularly drank. Some of the older boys would spar up to Charlie in the mornings and he would trade punches readily. His horny hands invariably persuaded his adversaries to break off the engagement.

Before morning school some children would wander down to the chute where from an iron pipe water still flows, constantly curving forcefully downward, opposite Glimsters Farm. There they drank, squirted their fellows, or played about in the gravel which was carried down by the water.

But you would always see two girls one on each side of Mrs Spratt's door, and when she came out they would help her down the steps and arm her along to school. Thus a halfpenny was earned, but I do not think the money was valued half as much as the prestige that went with the job.

At nine o'clock Mr Painter cut short all pre-school activities by ringing the bell that hung from a turret on the school. That brought everyone in line; the Infants by their porch door, and the girls and boys in their respective playgrounds. All walked through porches into the classrooms, except a couple of children whose job it was to pick up any litter.

In the Infant Room, following a hymn and a prayer, there was scripture for a good deal of the period from nine o'clock till a quarter to eleven. Table drills and sums followed to fill up the

The chute

first session, and afterwards the charts about mats and cats and reading carried us up to dinner.

Mrs Spratt was old; but Mrs Spratt was timeless. Mrs Spratt had taught all the children from way back. Her late husband had been the Head of Kentisbeare school. Then it filtered through: "Mrs Spratt is leaving. Mrs Spratt is retiring!" I couldn't believe it. But it happened. The old lady who loved us – yes, loved us I feel sure, in spite of all the tantalising – was soon to leave the classroom. The dark dresses, the beads, the ear-rings, the precise comb and strapped shoes would be no longer there for anyone to contemplate.

And as I think back on this, one incident stands out possibly more than any other in my remembrances of teacher. We were sitting on chairs in front of the blackboard, chanting at some chart or other. Mrs Spratt was looking at the board and then back at us. All at once, a little blonde girl stood up, pulled her knickers down and pulled her dress up to reveal a rather plump tummy. I was puzzled.

A boy explained: "If you say, 'Take your knickers down!' she will." Several of us proved this theory, and the young lady was up and down like a yo-yo. Then the inevitable happened, and as the timing went awry Mrs Spratt got a full frontal just as she turned around to us. That did it! The little blonde shopped us and we tried to shop each other. There was a fair shindig, with Mr Painter involved.

I hope the reader will not think I have recalled this to drag sex along to spice these memories. It merely seems so whimsical now, and when I see the erstwhile little blonde, I smile. I wonder if she remembers the incident. Somehow I don't like to ask her.

I don't suppose the foregoing exhibition had anything to do with our teacher's retirement. But inevitably, the day came. Mrs Spratt; Miss Spratt we always called her; left, and afterwards we used to wave to her as she sat in the window seat of her terraced cottage up the steps.

Who would come? Several! They all seemed so very young compared to our former teacher. They seemed so *lively* to me, and I remember I thought one, Miss Bending, was pretty.

Then along came Miss Christie.

MISS CHRISTIE, who was in her thirties, had rather a pale oval face. I used to think she looked Spanish. She had a quiet manner, and I remember she was very keen on nature study, giving lessons about the parts of flowers, writing up such words as pistil and calyx. I felt we were really beginning to learn things, and I daresay it was my enthusiasm that caused me to be a favourite with teacher, to the extent that some of the children teased me about it.

Another factor that brought me nearer to Miss Christie had to do with a prophecy made as Dennis and I were returning across the fields from the allotment with Mother, where we had been egg-collecting and cleaning out poultry houses.

On the outward journey Dennis went to climb over a gate, which was not properly hinged, and fell forward on top of him. There was immediate and loud bawling, which Dennis was good at, while Mother and I had quite a job lifting the wooden gate off him. On the return journey came the prophecy: "Don't run down over that bank! You will break your leg!"

I disobeyed the instruction, and fulfilled the prophecy; except that it was my arm and not my leg that was badly fractured. My arm pained, grew swollen, and hung heavily down. Slowly, we all made for home, and then there was a search for someone to take me to Exeter Hospital. Only a few folk had cars, of course, and it was some time before Fred Manning, a friend of Father's, drove up in his canvas-roofed jalopy and did the transportation. I learned in later years that because of this excitement Mother had a miscarriage.

As for me, in due course I went back to school with my arm in a sling and fairly well subscribed with boils. It was a low period, shall I say, and Miss Christie was very sympathetic and considerate.

I feel sure, though, that I also gained favour through the stories I wrote.

One day, we were invited to write about a picture I have mentioned earlier, in which children were picking primroses, and a squirrel sat in the branches of a tree. I found I could make a lot of that subject, and my attempt was shown to Mr Painter and, I believe, to the Rev. E. S. Chalk, who came to talk to Miss

Christie and the class. I remember another story about the cuckoo that was thought meritorious; and teacher wanted to see what I was writing on subjects she gave, almost before I had finished the job.

I remember how pleased Miss Christie was by the way we responded to the examining of the Diocesan Inspector. We chopped our hands through the air and properly guillotined his questions. At the end of the process the Inspector, whose bald dome I decided looked like an egg, was as bucked as he was exhausted. And Miss Christie's eyes lit up with a light you do not often see.

Miss Christie had a gold watch. That was quite unusual. She also showed us some rubies she had. I think that had to do with King Solomon.

But the following memory stands out. One January day we came into the classroom and found her drawing on the blackboard, with great concentration. We all sat and watched. What was it? It was a face; a lady's face, I decided after a while But the artist began to draw another face at the back of the profile she had drawn. Actually, she was sketching Janus, the Roman god.

A tittering began and swelled into a kind of jeering, raucous chorus. The artist went on, until . . . suddenly she spun round, and lectured us firmly about our rudeness. I suspect that everyone felt shattered and ashamed. Very likely I was affected the most of all, and I worried for days about the incident, wondering if Teacher had heard my contribution: me, with my special status! What was Miss Christie thinking of *me* ?

However, when the summer came, the charabanc to the sea was rather full and I sat — can you guess? I was pleased in one way, though realising all the same that extra teasing lay surely ahead.

Meanwhile, around the classroom little pieces of card were pinned up. They informed us that the a sound began apple, and there were pictures of apples, bats, cats and suchlike. I realise now that the frieze was designed to put a phonic ingredient into our reading diet. The c-a-t charts and chants of the so-called alphabetic system of reading were fading away in Kentisbeare.

Miss Christie was a splendid teacher. She moved from lodgings in the village to the hamlet of Dulford and walked to-and-fro school with the children each day.

Then at the end of the summer term, she was getting ready to go away with her father, when she received a letter from a nephew she was going to visit during the holiday. (Years later a man at the Four Horse Inn told me.)

Excitedly, she read the letter. Then she sat down, fell ill, and in a few hours was dead.

I heard she had died – but I could not believe. It wasn't true. But it was.

There was no Miss Christie when school started.

She had been taken a long way by hearse to her long home. And so she passed over and all the trumpets sounded for her on the other side. Surely they did! But none sounded in Kentisbeare.

CHAPTER 3

Standard I

WAS THERE ever a child who did not wish to get out of the 'baby' room: to leave the world of little chairs and tables, 'half' books, and nibbled pencils given out each day?

In Standard I, there were desks and text books, pens, ink, and joined writing — the same as the grown-ups did. There was also, in my case, Miss Howe. Miss Howe was really young — like my Aunt Nell, I thought. Scented and dressed in a careful fashion, she seemed so fresh and pretty. She was a pupil teacher, and a good deal of the work she did with us seemed to come out of a notebook that was always close at hand.

I reckon Mr Painter must have said to her, "Now Miss Howe, your first job is to concentrate on the looped style of handwriting!" Horrible bronze pointed instruments were dished out, and a boy filled the inkwells from a 'deformed' teapot that had a spout at right-angles to the handle. Then the torture started. You made big letters in the air, and at a later stage you copied a particular symbol from the board into a blue notebook that was given over to writing — or penmanship, as reports called it. As you copied, poking the pen through the paper every now and then, Miss Howe came around and either sat alongside or leaned over to make any necessary adjustments. In my case, there were plenty of adjustments to be made, and it was then that you really noticed the scent. I know the battle of the looped writing went on each day for several weeks until most of us were largely cured of the zig-zags and sausage loops, etc. Then you had periodic practices, and any imperfect letter was culled from whatever work you did and written down by Teacher to be copied along a line.

Once the looped emphasis had ceased, I began to settle in, and keep up with the best of the twenty-odd children in the class.

Mental arithmetic and spellings were daily events, and there were frequent exercises in a 'Fundamental English' book. At these aspects of classwork I was keen, and got good results.

When it came to composition — free writing they call it today — I was rather nobbled, as some of Miss Howe's titles were not friendly to my mode of expression. I recall one composition was 'My Favourite Cake', and when brother Dennis encountered the same title the following year, he is reputed to have written thus: 'My favourite cake is a chocolate cake. But Mother can't afford them and we eats dough cakes.' However, I am pretty sure that Miss Howe, a conscientious, thoroughly competent teacher, had the idea of restricting one's output of words and getting some commas and full stops included in the right places — sensible strategy of which a good many of today's teachers seem either ignorant or disdainful.

Our teacher had a weekly poetry spot and I always enjoyed the poems she read out and wrote up for us to copy:

All along the backwater,
Through the rushes tall,
Ducks are a-dabbling,
Up tails all!

I remember that poem by Kenneth Grahame was one of the first we included in our poetry books.

Singing entered into things, and we rehearsed the words of 'Strawberry Fair', 'Begone Dull Care', 'Golden Slumbers' and other songs, in the class-room.

Besides our poetry books, there was another little blue book into which we pressed flowers and labelled them, as a sequel to nature lessons.

Thus rolled the regular, formal sequence, and in between times I looked, when it was safe, at pictures high along the wall. There, Caxton, The Princes in The Tower, Hereward, and a number of others looked down at us all. Those characters intrigued me, and I am sure my interest in history came through these watchers from the high frieze.

But there were days when I had to forget them, for examination time had arrived.

On one occasion I collected ninety marks overall, and somehow

I got to know this. I must have been one of the first to be totted up, for I listened to Teacher as she muttered the scores of rivals. Once I heard her get up to eighty-nine, and then stop. My detective work was accurate, and it was confirmed that I was top and that my cousin, Betty Chamberlain, was second. That constituted two victories in one, so to speak, and when I took my report home, I was doubly acclaimed. Gran Goff at Guddiford had to walk the tightrope as a result of such a photo-finish, whilst Gran Rugg was exultant. It was the only time I came top overall at Kentisbeare School, or in any other for that matter.

Miss Howe promised me a prize and I reminded her tactfully of this from time to time. She eventually gave me a yellow magazine-cum-book. I am afraid I was rather falling out of favour by that time. I will tell you about it.

ON ONE half-day each week Miss Howe went somewhere else to teach, and Mr Painter had the extra job of looking in to see how we were getting on with the work left behind for us to do.

No doubt we stuck to our tasks well enough for a week or so, but before long we began to run around the room and generally play about. The result was upbraiding and caning every week, with the Head really cutting his stick across our hands. During the punishment we winced, and afterwards succoured the afflicted palm for a bit: and then went back to our unscheduled activities.

A certain knot of boys shared all the stick that was going, and I have no doubt that Miss Howe was told the names of the criminals. Hence, when 'Derrick Rugg put out his tongue' one day, I must have been already in the criminal records file. I recall that Miss Howe had just told me off about some minor thing, and I had thought no more of it. Then I saw four girls had their hands raised.

"Derrick Rugg put his tongue out to you, Miss!" offered one girl gleefully. Why she should have said this, I have never been able to fathom. Perhaps it was because I was much better at lessons than the obsequious Lizzy female.

"Did you?" asked Miss Howe.

"No!" I said.

William Leatt *c.* 1936

Jimmy Vinnicombe with the Manfields, traction engine and reed comber

The little girl in blue,
in fancy dress

Mrs Spratt

Miss Christie and her class
Derrick in front of Miss Christie
Dennis, front row 2nd from right

"He did, Miss!" several girls voluntarily emphasised.

"I did not!" I insisted.

But the more vehemently I defended myself, the more the girls seemed to clamour for my blood. It was incredible.

"Perhaps," I offered, "I was wetting my lips!" I explained that I did this sometimes.

Whether this was taken as a half admission of guilt, I do not know, but Mr Painter was called for and the interrogation started again from scratch. I can see him now, standing weighing things up, fiddling with his cane: he had brought his cane, I noticed. To be fair, he seemed unable to decide whether I was guilty or not, but after some hesitation I was caned — for nothing.

How I resented that, but how I wished I could get my own back on the lying girls who positively gloated over the outcome of their enterprise! I am sure that getting fixed in the way I have described first upset my relationship with the girls of my age, and put me at odds with teachers. Certain girls would say I had been talking or doing something wrong whenever they could. Often it was trumped up, but I got clobbered just the same. After a while, I took to punching the girls for their pains, for which I was labelled a bully. More caning!

Also, there was the affair of the blotting paper. I had lost the official issue, and whether I was told to replace it, I do not remember. But I did get another piece.

Aunt Nell worked in Miller's Stores, and I used to go in sometimes when I had a penny to spend, noticing when Aunt was behind the counter, as Miss Miller was regarded as tight; would "skin a flint", according to Gran Rugg. In such circumstances, it was logical to assume that the most favourable time to shop was when the assistant was present.

"Have you by any chance got a piece of blotting paper?" was my unusual request. There was some conversation, followed by a hunt until a piece was found in a box under the counter. I offered the twopence I had.

"Put that away!" Aunt Nell said. "It's rather a dirty piece." So I did, and took my 'purchase' along to school.

Where had I got it? Miss Howe wanted to know when she saw

it. I had bought it, I told her and everyone who enquired.

Where had I bought it?

Then I began to splutter and stall, fearing that if I came clean, Aunt Nell would be in the soup, get the sack — or something. But at last, I had to relate the train of events; and I don't know whether I was believed or not, for I had tied myself in knots emphasising the shop-soiled nature of the goods I had acquired. Did they think I had pinched it in school? I could feel the doubt and suspicion.

The Coronation didn't help matters either, for it meant country dancing, which I hated at the best of times. I couldn't master the one-two-three-up, polka torture and, in any event I didn't want to be involved with girls whose hair I would rather have pulled. I sulkily cavorted around, and tried to get Mother to bale me out. But it was no good, and I was pulled and shoved through nine or so dances on the Rectory Lawn, to gain more dirty looks and black marks. 'Picking up Pea Pods!' Ugh!

So whilst I can say I learned a great deal in Miss Howe's class, in the field of personal relationships I lost ground. I felt aggrieved,

Miller's stores

resentful, and justifiably vengeful. I am sure teachers thought I was developing a chip on my shoulder.

The foregoing events cast a shadow across some of my days at Kentisbeare School.

May I leave the classroom? No, not for the usual reason: for a breath of morning air!

WHEN the weather was fine, most of us endeavoured to get to school as early as possible in order to kick around a tennis ball in the playground.

My journey was barely a quarter of a mile compared to the two miles or so of some of my fellows, and I usually set off early enough to be able to dawdle along, alone, or with others; I did not mind how it was. I used to climb upon a wall, along a gate and then down the hill to Catford Court, where when the air was still there was an aroma of tobacco laid by Mr Hill on the way to his workshops in Back Lane, as Gran called it. Sometimes one met the carpenter, and unlike most of the crotchety older men, he invariably spoke to every child by name at every meeting.

Catford Court was a gathering point; a kind of social-sports centre. Three houses formed a terrace there, which looked out on to a part-cobbled, gravelly court. In one of the houses lived the six Goff children and in the end place, Harold Leatt. In the middle a lively, imaginative girl called Lovis held court. She used to have a list of boys she held in esteem, and every now and then would indicate with an impish twinkle whereabouts you were placed. I was second for a time.

From Catford Court onwards it was likely that a group of ten or a dozen children would be found proceeding to school. I would have to look in for a second or two on Gran Rugg, and then go on to Mr Leatt's workshop. There in the thirties it was bang! bang! bang! all the day, as it was the poultry era, when all farmers and many other folk had hens. I have been told that Kentisbeare had the highest fowl population of any other parish in the country, and certainly the cluckings and crowings every morning came strongly from all points of the compass.

We would always look in at Mr Leatt's workshop to check on things, and old Mr Leatt would be tolerant for a little while. He would ask us 'school' questions. Then he would tell us abruptly to get along. Harry, one of his sons, seemed almost always to be painting carts or wagons, and Fred, the other son, small, quick, and thoughtful, seemed taken over by problems of the trade as he hummed away, pencil behind ear. Old Mr Leatt was often found clouting the bottom out of a cart, and Gran Rugg used to say, "He likes that. They give him jobs like that," meaning, I took it, that he was old and possessed no desire for finicky work, or had perhaps lost his finer touch.

Going forward, one passed the petrol pumps where petrol, including ROP, was less than a shilling a gallon; and then climbed the cobbled path bordering Village Hill which was also called Priest Hill. Here I regularly felt compelled to count my steps at the steepest part, where the bier house was passed on the left and the churchyard on the right.

As apple time approached, the Beauty of Bath tree in Miss Miller's garden did not go unnoticed, and if Paddy, the Landlord of the Wyndham Arms, chanced to be looking fixedly out of the

Catford Court

bar window, we would stop and cheekily return his stare.

The square with its horse-chestnut tree saw the converging of the clans and the dividing up to shops, chute, the smithy, or playground.

On fine days, a ball or tin could have been kicked to school, and at one time there was a great craze for tops. When the weather grew cold the iron hoops came out, along with wheels and tyres. Gran Rugg reluctantly let me have Father's hoop, so I was properly equipped, but some of the boys got their own back by being 'way out' and persuading the strangest and largest rolling stock they could find along the by-ways. In season conkers were much in evidence, and there were all sorts of theories on how to achieve all-conquering conkers, including baking, keeping for two years, and soaking in vinegar.

Obtaining a conker was quite a problem. The tree in the square was unproductive, and the nearest fruitful chestnuts were at the Rectory, where Mr Pollard, the gardener, was OK one day and liverish the next. Three other days were in dark Dulford Wood, mysterious to all save the Dulford and Kerswell children. The only other source was one tree in front of The Priory, an historical place close to Kerswell. So, to be assured of sufficient ammunition in conker battles, you had to wait for and butter up the suppliers when they came at morning, and it was then that the boys who brought sandwiches, bananas, apples, etc., would exmaine their tins in their satchels and do some swopping. There was little doubt that Mr Moulding, the smith, was being cannily observed, as his box of horse nails was closely relevant to boys and their conkers. The smith was alert though, and fast to award a clip around the ear to any apprehended malefactor. I speak from experience.

Before school, boys would chat about the arrival of a thresher on a farm, and arrange to visit it at dinnertime if the tackle was anywhere handy.

That, roughly, was the scene up to the bell, when we would go from various points to our lines.

Mr Tytler, plus-foured and Peterson-piped, would sometimes remonstrate from the gate of The Retreat by the school, about our sins of omission or commission regarding noise, litter and so on. No-one took much notice, I'm afraid.

In the clutches of school, we slogged on till dinnertime.

DINNER TIME, which began at twelve o'clock, did not feature the School Meals Service.

Out of the gate on the dot went a helter-skelter of boys, with the girls suitably less wild. In the lead for some years was Tommy Tidball who lived next to me. He rushed home, ate his dinner, and returned to school at his fastest speed. Close behind Tom was Louis Jefferies, who stayed with Gran Goff at Guddiford Mills. He had around a half-mile to cover, and he also ran all the way out and back.

Dennis and I used to have our dinner in Silver Street at Gran Rugg's, for most of the time I was at Kentisbeare School. At other times we went home, and although I tried and tried, I could not put one on Tom Tidball. Some children had relations with whom they could dine; notably the little girl in blue I mentioned, but a large group had to delve into their tins, if they had not dug too deeply at the morning break. The only change for them came with the arrival of pasties from the bakery. These were ordered first thing and arrived hot — and sometimes a little overdone — after twelve.

But wherever food was taken, by half-past twelve a re-assembly was well under way, with dinner-break activities in prospect. Perhaps there would be a sectionalised affair, with some boys playing horses and driving each other round at the end of strawcord, while others went 'chasing' all around the village. I liked the latter game, as I seemed to have the special guile that was called for. When I was being chased, I ran out of school and then stood behind some object. My pursuers invariably charged on and I merely walked back to the playground and gloated over my cunning and the consequent fruitless exertions of my pursuers.

Occasionally there was an emphasis on football or cricket, depending on the availability of necessary gear, but if the morning's exchange of information had thrown up a threshing machine in the vicinity, off went the majority of the boys, especially if the beautifully polished Queen Mary had arrived at

Cotter's Farm. That was strange, when you come to think of it, for there was nothing to do except to stand and stare; and if the men amid all the flapping of belts, throbbing of the drum and hum of fly-wheel could have waved a wand, I daresay we would have found ourselves in their stations of torture.

There was always something to see at the smithy, with several horses often waiting as patiently as their carters. Or one could see the smith rush out to bond an iron tread on a cart-wheel that Mr Hill had wheeled up from his shop.

In the autumn term there were scrumping expeditions, which often resulted in complaints from farmers and warnings from Mr Painter.

Another activity that started in the summer term and drew most of the boys and a lot of girls into its compass was catching minnows in the brook that ran past the school, or in the leat that once served the redundant backshot wheel across the common. You placed jam-jars amid the water weeds and left them there a

Minnowing in the mill stream

day or so for the little fish to swim into. We would exult at the capture of a red-throat and stow our catch away until collection after school. We took them home then and put them in larger containers, but in spite of stones and weed to stimulate the habitat, I cannot recall minnows lasting more than a few days.

Mixed up with fishing were paddling, jumping across channels, pushing one another in the water, and making dams, and suchlike. You would often see a boy sitting, wringing away, trying to beat the water out of his socks; and just before one o'clock by the church clock, there was a procession to the ablutions, i.e. the chute. We were warned from time to time about the open sewers of Kentisbeare, and the risks we took of contracting this or that, for many drains and lavatories were piped directly into the brook, but I'm afraid the admonitions went in at one ear and out of the other.

As I have said, the fishers among us retrieved our catch at home-time from the hide-aways by the insalubrious water-courses. But unlike the men of Galilee we heard of in scripture, there was no profit of any kind: no money in it.

HOW to get some money was a good question. There wasn't any such thing as regular pocket money, and the gaining of pennies was a chancy process.

Sometimes there was somebody's letter to be posted: "Here! Hold this letter like this!" instructed old Mrs Potter, placing the address against the palm in a useless attempt to foil curiosity. For this a penny was forthcoming, which seemed to be divided in the lady's mind, allowing a halfpenny for successful posting and a halfpenny for not casing the address.

Mrs Bragg was an occasional customer, but she would say at the completion of the posting or shopping, "I daresay you are hungry! I expect you could eat a piece of cake, couldn't you?" Hence, a piece of fruit cake was sliced off — though we would rather have had a penny. Mother didn't like the "I expect you are hungry" bit, but also instructed us to refuse any coins of the realm. We did make some show on this, holding the hand half out at the same time.

Mrs Potter would occasionally beckon: "Mr Potter wants

someone to turn the grindstone while he sharpens his scythe." A time and price was mentioned, and later you walked along with a white-bearded morose old man to the grindstone in Mr Hill's orchard. Hardly a word was said as you worked away and the sharpener leaned over his tool. Every now and then the great sandstone disc was given a drink, and it seemed ages before the cutting edge was keen enough. The shilling was well earned.

Cobble-stones were worth sixpence. The equipment needed was a stubby kitchen knife, a sack to kneel on, and a bucket for the weeds, which had to be scraped and prised from their comfortable niches. There was a good deal of competition for that job, which played havoc with fingers. Also our employers, knowing there were other weeders in the wings, demanded the highest standard. However, a workmanlike effort meant further contracts, and in my case I had Aunt Nell. She seemed to collect boy friends readily, and I assumed she wished her suitors to see a tidy frontage at Guddiford Mills. This meant a patch of cobbles to weed, besides other weeding and brushing.

"I don't believe you are working!" Aunt Nell would shout out a couple of times each contract, from somewhere inside the parlour window.

'How the devil do you know?' I used to think. 'How can you tell without looking to see?' Also, I thought to myself, she ought to have known that I wanted the sixpence, and besides, there was the inspection at the end. I came to realise that the hollering-out feature had become habitual, and I concluded that she probably didn't realise she was holding forth. She wasn't the least bit tight, anyway.

My brother secured a daily contract at Bishop's Farm, cracking linseed cake. You had to put the quite heavy slabs into the top of the crusher and then wind away on a handle. It was all right with 'green' cake, but not so good after cake had been stacked long enough to harden.

Treading hay ricks was a job that boys were given, when the idea was to keep walking alongside and behind the rickmaker, who would instantly spot any tendency to dream or take root. One day I thought whilst in attendance on Mr Tom Blackmore, when no pay had been stipulated and the only evident advantage was a drink out of the lid of the great tea can, that it would be an idea to ask if I could bring a mate along, to relieve the monotony.

The rickmaker stopped, cleared his throat and said:

"One boy's a boy,
Two boys half a boy,
Three boys no boy at all!"

I gathered that company was out.

At harvest time, there was a chance to turn sheaves, which meant picking up sheaves as they were pitched on to the rick and pushing them across, butt first, to the maker of the stack. There was never any precise, hourly reward for a task that could be hellish when you were involved with a rick builder who wanted slide-rule service, or one who wasn't getting enough cider to mull his irritability. Uncle Arthur belonged to the meticulous variety and would give a running commentary, "By me leg! Too far behind!", on practically every sheaf. However, at haytime and harvest anyone could have a swig at the cider jar, and I remember Mr Retter having such a large stone container that I had to rest the bottom on a ladder rung and draw the neck downwards to drink.

Then, as anyone got to nine or ten, farmers or their men would stop and ask if you would like to 'earn a bob' leading a horse at horse-hoe. Well, yes – and no. Farm horses were so clumsy that you wondered where their great feet would land next, and there was the very real chance that a surly man would be guiding the implement and would holler at every deviation. Also, some horses were very hardmouthed and would drag and pull you down, and then rush wildly out at the ends of rows. It wasn't a job I liked, except when I operated with Granfer Goff, or Len Vincent. The latter told jokes and laughed like hell, in an infectious way. Grandfather, besides being tolerant and not given to rushing, possessed boy psychology. "We will give the horse a blow and have a drink at the end of the next row!"

Filling-in between the more substantial night-time, Saturday, or holiday jobs, meant fetching the odd bucket of water, pound of candles, or gallon of paraffin. There was Gran Goff's shopping at twopence a week and sometimes Jack Salisbury, who lived in at Guddiford Mills, wanted his boots taken to or collected from Walter Leyman, the cobbler. The boot-mender, 'Squeaker' behind his back, would tend to go on a bit; "Look, boy, this is kip leather, K-I-P" and so on, and he seemed proud if he could demonstrate a giant machine by stitching a boot or shoe. Jack Salisbury was a good, immediate paymaster.

Paddy O'Brien, the Irish landlord of the Wyndham Arms, who had two moods, convivial or very prickly, had to have water in his loft tanks, and there was the chance for a couple of boys to earn threepence each, wrestling with a stiff pump handle until water came out of a spout on the roof. It was hard work, but more 'profitable' than listening to the Rev. Hodges' Sunday morning sermons.

Another job arose through Bill Lane, who had the authority to recruit and pay a gang of boys to put sawdust along the lines of the football pitch on Friday nights or Saturday mornings; although the weather could be unpleasant, the threepence counted.

In season, old men would pull out potatoes deftly enough with two-tined diggers, but were disinclined, through status or stiffness perhaps, to bend down and gather them. I have walked into an autumn field where Ned Newberry had been digging and wondered if it were possible to make any impression on never-ending lines. Pay, via Mr Retter, Ned's boss, could not be estimated in advance.

Getting some coins to put in trouser or waistcoat pockets was an altogether chancy business. I collected twenty pennies one week. Twenty pennies!

Amidst all the uncertainty, I did gather, through some of the things Mother said, that one or two of our relations were well-to-do. The trouble is they were the distant ones, i.e. the ones we never saw.

May I go back to the classroom?

CHAPTER 4

Towards The Top Class

I SHOULD tell you that the school was 'decapitated' when I was nine years old. It sounds a painful operation, but it only involved taking the children of eleven-and-over three miles by charabanc-bus to Cullompton Senior School. At that time, various alterations were made to the school, whereby the big room lost its parting curtains and was furnished with a folding wood-and-glass screen.

I found myself in Mrs Painter's class where there was a big table for needlework and a large tortoise stove on which saucepans (full of laundry?) were sometimes placed. There was also a piano.

I was seated with my brother Dennis for a while, and that caused a problem in that he seemed to think I ought to be on call when he couldn't do his sums. I was torn by this. On the one hand, I knew that I would be in trouble if I helped him and I also felt that, as I had experienced no difficulty where he was all at sea, he ought to be able to cope. The outcome was the odd dig or a gesture of refusal to help, and Mrs Painter moved me for doing this, so I was in the soup anyway, and what she said to me also rankled.

However, I did not stay in that class long, as children were promoted at any time during the year, depending on progress in English and Maths.

But I have several memories, amongst them Mrs Painter's tenacity; yes, that's the word; over singing. I can see her now, marching jauntily across the front of the class, giving a spirited rendering of 'Strawberry Fair' to get us in the mood.

"Wandering minstrels thought up such ditties," she said, and the 'ri-fol, ri-fol', we were told, was put in so as to allow the singer-composer time to think up the next line. At any rate, we sang about the health of His Majesty, a lawyer who fancied a farmer's daughter, and a maiden who got up early to sing in the valley.

Singing would start as a reading exercise and then proceed bit by bit until we couldn't sing a bit properly, or were judged to be lacking in enthusiasm. Then the 'fierce' mantle that I had heard about before I even started school was assumed all right, and we might have been found with three fingers down our throats jerked back in our seats, going up and down and all over the place in response to a pointer and a dun tonic-solfa chart that was hung on the ear of the easel. That was when Mrs Painter grew 'as red as a turkey-cock' and became oblivious of school-time and play-time. But she made us sing. In the middle of a song, she could somehow hammer a note twice, as a corrective, and bash along with the phrase all in the same movement. During all the twenty-eight years I have served schools, I have never come across such drive, determination, and peculiuar skill, and when I recall a Nativity Play at Kentisbeare, in which eight or nine children of eleven years and under sang solos in carols, I wonder and I wonder.

Apart from that sort of expertise, a teacher at that time had to push us through the arithmetic and English books, associated tests being as regular as clockwork. Marks were recorded in books made during handwork lesson, and each week someone was top of the class. Sometimes we called out our marks, and everyone used to smile at Seward Webber, who would shout out high marks at top volume, reducing to very low power when he had not been so successful. I rarely, if ever, found myself top of the heap, and I used to be annoyed over this as I felt a system of 'neatness marks' acted against me.

Nature study was a feature of Mrs Painter's teaching, and she used to tell us what she had seen on her regular walks around Croyle and other places. Of course, with all the children footing it to school, many matters of interest among flora and fauna were noted by the walkers, and there was no shortage of material to sit on window ledges or in nature corners. Reflecting on that, one regrets the great buses of today that incarcerate, and pre-empt the interest of the great outside. In my schooldays, we knew where the sweet violets hid behind the patent green of brome grasses; we knew where wild strawberries grew and we knew the most prolific nut-trees. We knew where finches nested, where 'battle heads' dreamed under stones, where the ragged robin grew... We discovered so many things, quite often by accident.

Albeit, on went the table drills, with 'twenty two yards make one chain', etc. There was a time when I thought there was little value in some of the daily stints, particularly the alphabetic chanting – about cats and mats, you will remember. I still have educational reservations, especially about the latter routine, but circumstances were so different in those days. There were not the books and other aids that tend to clutter up today's classrooms. There was no TV, and just the beginnings of radio. I never saw any advisers, remedial teachers, or other supporting staff, and there could not have been much in the way of encouragement or refreshment for the workers at the 'chalkface'. So folk like Mrs Spratt and Miss Howe found themselves *invested* with numbers of country children, a good proportion of whom were not bright. On a restricted site, with few props, such teachers had to ring the changes to keep us occupied and educated. They did this; and more. The drills I once thought tiresome, if not useless, were conditioning us into a work routine which we were going to need.

I often feel that such discipline ought to be more in evidence today.

WHEN I found myself in Mr Painter's room I felt I had really arrived, for not only was I in the top class, I was going to be taught by a man. Nearly all, if not all, children look forward to the end of petticoat government.

To begin with, I did what all children surely do; I studied the room, where we occupied rows of double desks, except for two girls who sat aside facing our profiles. Can you guess the identity of one of the girls? All I will say is that I was still mutely in thrall, and when the top group of two had poetry to learn and recite, my eyes and ears were especially attuned:

'A wet sheet and a flowing sea...'

Up in front of the class was a large cupboard, behind which sat, when he sat, the Head. On his left on a special shelf was a radio, and on the immediate right a small tortoise stove. At the side of the room were shelves which constituted the Devon County Library, with the small school handbell consorting in a niche with a large ink jar. There was also a large cupboard, a globe, and a yellowish cane with a knob for head-tapping. That was how I review things.

Mr Painter, a wearer of tweed suits, was always redolent of tobacco. He occasionally sent boys to get Turf tobacco from the Post Office, and when he marked my book, his fingers I noted, were brown from cork tips.

He, like all the teachers I had known, gave priority to the basics. We spent a long period in the mornings doing sums, and there was plenty of formal English work. It may seem eccentric or even heretical to some, these days, but work was marked daily, and corrections followed. If you had not done your stint, or had not come up to scratch, then playtime could be forgotten.

Mr Painter would surely have been considered under stress by today's standards for he had plenty on his plate, as they say, apart from school. He was an avid reader of the classics and historical novels, and it was he who kept the rainfall records and drew the annual graphs. There was a greenhouse to look after, beehives, and a sizeable garden which was nurtured with extraordinary skill. He went to church and choir practice regularly. He was on the Church Council, and rang occasionally with the ringers, whom he tried unsuccessfully to convert to method ringing, in which the pattern of 'changes' has to be understood and memorised, instead of being read from a card. The football club was launched by Archie, and he had played until he transferred to support. He turned out with the lads at cricket, and small boys like us always said: "Hard luck, sir," when he was out. Mr Painter cycled to collect National Savings; Mr Painter was asked to say a few words on this or that occasion; Mr Painter was to the fore at flower show, fête, fair, and so on. Mr Painter also taught us unremittingly, interestingly, and with a skill that looked easy.

Perhaps there is one aspect where he could, or should, have

had more perception. It concerned the antagonistic group of girls I mentioned earlier, for the persecution-retaliation cycle went on right up the school. Whenever the Head went out of the room, I was reported, often quite wrongly, to have been talking or to have thumped some 'angelic' female. Hence, my bully label became more and more firmly attached and I was 'a bad example to the evacuees', when they came, and also 'the reason we were fighting the war'. The Head grew to resent me, I know, and I also grew resentful and sulky, feeling that I was in a patent trap. There I was, the only boy at that age level, up to my neck in it, and I confess that I still wonder why no-one rumbled things instead of giving me lecture, cane, lecture, cane . . .

However, in the warmth of relationships formed and sustained as I grew into my teens and then went onto Saint Luke's, which had been Mr Painter's college, the bitterness of the early years melted away.

I remember his stories about the First World War, in which the Head had been a lieutenant, supervising the telephone that linked the trenches. He told us of comradeship and bravery, and also inadequacy, when boy soldiers cried at night for 'Mother'. We were told of young lads overloaded with rum 'going over the top' blowing hunting horns, and being picked up later on, dead, with magazine covers still in place on their rifles.

Talks of boyhood near the Tamar were a speciality; of strawberries and a big pool which everyone said was bottomless, until A. E. Painter dived in and collected stones from the bottom. Swinging the lamp? Then there was the 'how we won the cup' story. Several times I heard the Head begin like Alice at the beginning and detail through; how Charlie Moulding, the blacksmith, did that, and goalie Edward Goff, my uncle, did the other. In the end, the Fox Cup, we learned, was secured and celebrated, and it was said that on that one occasion Archie was somewhat tipsy. The trouble about the story was that for several years I thought the cup so glorified must have been the FA Cup! I really did; and that was not the only misapprehension I caught in the Top Class, for I became convinced for some years, following a poetry lesson, that poets had to have a licence. Well, some ought!

A Kentisbeare lane

Kentisbeare Post Office

Harvesting

Kentisbeare Football Team and the Fox Cup

"How many of your fathers could do this?" would be the rhetorical question during regular PT lessons in the playground. And the aftermath would sometimes be a search for coins that had left pockets during the particular agility exhibited.

"Bowl straight – and a good length!" was the instruction when our coach came down at playtime or after lunch, and we were shown how to take guard, hold the bat and use our feet; how to push the ball into certain sectors marked by chalk marks on wall or fence. 'Through the covers' was a good score and 'past the bowler', counted. Over into the garden was 'out, man, out!' For our mentor was concerned with style and concentration, not with the fracturing of cloches or annoying of bees.

Mr Painter was well versed in nature, and I recall that he told us a lot about bees, and amphasised kindness to animals, sometimes through poetry.

> I hear a sudden cry of pain!
> There is a rabbit in a snare;
> Now I hear the cry again
> But I cannot tell from where...
> Little one! Oh! Little one!
> I am searching everywhere.

Thus the days went by, and also to go was the 'Piers Plowman' history books. The first story I had read in those dark green trasuries was with Mrs Spratt in the Infants Room. It told of the elopement of Helen and the Siege of Troy, and I can see now the picture of a vessel on the first page. Then it was 'Romulus and Remus', and 'Horatius', and 'Alexander and Bucephalus' ... Why did 'Piers Plowman' have to go? I was angry about it, for I loved those stories.

Come Friday, the wireless was plugged in for 'Travel Talks'. They weren't very interesting to me, and my mind took flight to cricket pitches or cornfields.

CRICKET, from early years, had much to do with our spare time. First you needed a bat, and that came from a genuinely loose, or coaxed loose, bar of a gate. One end was shaped for the handle, and the bottom was sometimes rounded off. Most boys possessed bats of various dimensions and qualities.

The first cricket ground I can remember was Catford Court, where one had to compete for space with ducks, a fowl-house or two, a woodrick, and the pump house. The pitch was definitely not up to county standard, and the tennis ball bounced uncertainly on its way to the wicket which was an upright piece of timber built into the wall. There must often have been getting on for twenty boys and girls from whom sides were picked. A clout into the adjacent orchard meant six, and out!

In season and out of season, we congregated in the Court, tolerated by the householders. But as the years went on we gradually drew off to Mr Blackmore's little field at the back of Silver Park, among the thistles, where we used to play for hours.

The wicket was a stick overhung by a coat, or one of the reels that the electric man had left behind when they put the 'mains' in the council houses. Acquiring a ball or suitable missile was a continual problem, and it varied from sponge, tennis, cork, or plastic to wood. One large black plastic sphere lasted for a long

The view of Blackborough House

time before splitting into hemispheres; and a croquet ball was introduced in emergencies.

Thus we played, and as we played we kept our weather eye open. Months would go by, our uninvited occupation of the field seemingly accepted. Then the situation would radically change. Perhaps someone had been running about in Farmer Blackmore's mowing grass, had left a gate open, or had chased his horses. But whatever it was, an irate farmer would appear, and let us have it at top volume, lacing his peroration with talk of hidings, schoolmasters, and police, before issuing immediate orders to quit his field. After such a cataclysm, we had to find another pitch for a while, to effect a cooling-off period. Then we surreptitiously crept back, maintaining a super *qui vive* for a prescribed period, relaxing again until the next time a Morris Cowley stopped, or an ancient bicycle was placed firmly against the gate.

He was a pretty good sport though, Farmer Tom!

However, on Saturday mornings during the proper cricket season, you would not have seen us among the field thistles, or dashels, and sheeps' droppings. No, if there was a game at the Rectory, we would be anxiously sky watching; and we would sing if it was rainy:

Rain, rain go away,
Come again another day!

For all of us were dead keen on the real thing; and besides, there was a chance to knock around with a spare bat. So we urged the rain to keep off, and if it did we eagerly helped to cut the pitch with a hand-mower, gave a hand with the marking out, and scraped off any cow dabs.

During games, we watched the local heroes and aped their bowling actions. I tried Ray Hill's action for a bit and tried to work out how the elderly Mr Hodges could drive the ball miles across into Blackmore's field. He seemed to pat his bat on the ground as the poor, hapless bowler came up. Then the ball was up in the clouds, wishing I shouldn't wonder for a parachute.

Besides all this, one helped Mrs Milton to put tables under the appointed oak-tree, and then watched her arrange the refreshments. Then we hoped the players would not eat everything. They never did!

But apart from the battles fought by the village side, cricket had to give way to the lure of cornfields.

As August approached, the fields of winter oats, which would be the earliest to be sliced and bundled away by horse-drawn binders, were kept under general observation, while harvest information started to come in. Somebody would report on a probable starting date, by Farmer Morrish, say. Another would have information about the campaign readiness of an Albion or Massey Harris machine, and tension would increase as swathes were cut around the margins of fields.

Then one ecstatic day, the first machine actually sallied forth to mow down the legions of standing corn. Boys and girls with walking sticks, and cudgels fashioned by pocket knives, plus a number of dogs, followed the ungainly, packed-up binder down the lanes to the place of cutting, flailing and tying.

Before the operation could start the binder would have to be unpacked. Smaller iron wheels had to be taken off and inserted in different sockets at right angles to their road positions. The driving pole had to be changed, extra beaters bolted on, the big driving wheel wound down and a driving shaft inserted. Though it was never admitted, a few boys were needed to heave and pull, at wheel changing. After that, the cord was put in the cord tin and threaded through to the needle, the canvass that carried the corn were tightened, various adjustments were made, and it was in gear and away.

That was it, boys! If the binder was dutiful; didn't break a chain, and the tying gear behaved; the concentric journey was under way, and we followed the rattling machine round and round and round and round . . . In the course of our traipsing we were ready to help when the machine became choked by straw or to offer technical advice at a breakdown. At the end of our stint of circuits, we were as black as chimney sweeps from the dust shaken off corn, thistles, and poppies.

"Why do you have to get like that!" Mother said, despairingly, resignedly.

Well, there was a kind of competition as to who could go round the greatest number of times, and you stuck at it. You felt involved with the men, too. When you grew tired, or the labouring horses or their driver had a break, there were sheaves to sit upon, and in the wheatfields you could thresh out and eat corn.

Men walked mechanically around sitting up the corn into 'stitches', little houses of six or eight sheaves, and they talked happily, refreshing themselves from time to time at cans of tea or cider jars. Great toads lumbered along in the stubble, hundreds of small dull moths were a-flutter, and quaint spider-like harvestmen lifted themselves along, while the binder brought scarlet pimpernels to light, along with the yellow of fumitory and the delicate beauty of wild pansies. Big children kept their eye on smaller folk, to give mothers a welcome release, and regardless of shins bruised by the stubble and sheaf butts, we were as happy as larks.

As the island of uncut corn grew smaller and smaller, the rabbits must have rumbled that they were running out of time. One 'hero' would suddenly decide to run the gauntlet, pursued by hollering boys, girls, men, and dogs. The desperate creature would be hampered by sheaves, and that would determine a zig-zag progress towards the safety of surrounding banks. Dogs tore into pursuit only to be foiled by a change of direction, which meant they had to clap on their brakes and set their sights again. Sticks were thrown as the cacophany of yells increased.

There was, I used to fancy, about a fifty-fifty chance of a four-legged athletic rabbit making an escape. Others, chopped about by knives, dragged their mutilated half-selves away until the blood had drained and light faded from their eyes. But there was no sympathetic feeling for them, as we raced amidst the carnage and smashed and threw our cudgels of clumsy death, for come the end of the day we hoped the farmer would award us a respectable casualty that we could give to Mother, or better still, sell for a few pence, to Bessie Rowe, perhaps.

But oh, at the end of a day's rabbiting we were so indescribably dry. We would go to the nearest spring, stream, ditch, pump, or tank, and we would drink, drink and drink . . . the thirstiness and weariness were total.

But the next day, weather permitting, we would be off again

to the grime, sweat, gore, excitement, and community made patent in a cornfield.

We were likely to do a spot of scrumping on the way.

AS YOU walked alongside orchards in fruiting time, the apples bent down lower and lower, seeming to grin and beckon as you passed. Temptation welled. No-one was around as far as anyone could see, and what were a few boys among a million fruits? You stopped and all seemed silent, ominously silent. Was that a favourable thing or the lull before the storm? Was Farmer Tom, thumbsticked and adjacent, poised behind the bole of a tree ready to jump and rage before apprehending a boy, full-bosomed with plunder? Or was he not? Our heads peered through the gaps in the fence and the birds seemed to go on strike. Glances were exchanged that eventually became more concentrated on the brave, foolhardy, or easily led. The emotional pressure was intense!

If a lead was forthcoming, a gate or stile was cleared in low profile, and a crouching dash to the nearest tree preceded an all-systems-go stuffing operation. It always seemed that a fearsome, profane outburst was imminent, mixed up with the barking of dogs, and scuffling of leggings and boots.

Was that a Morris Cowley in the distance?

All being well, the syndicate ate all kinds of apples, sweet or sour, on principle, and it was best to keep quiet about any colic that followed.

One was always afraid that a misused farmer would come to see the Head; and sometimes that happened, for some farmers appeared to memorise, or perhaps photograph, their apple-trees, and noting one or two missing, take on the mantle of the Good Shepherd. It was nauseating, almost as nauseating as some of the cider apples collected on frantic scrumpings.

But the scrumping game was improved by a knowledge of the distribution of desirable apples. Mr Blackmore had three or four soft, sweet Plum Vidys; there was a very early apple in the Back Lane or Machine Orchard and a Beauty of Bath tree was only just over Miss Miller's garden wall. There were Pigs' Snouts in the orchard at Cotter's Farm and a free tree of tasteless apples by the pigs' houses at Bishop's Farm. Turning sheaves there meant all the apples you could munch, plus the tea can.

One way or another, we did not go short of apples, and I was especially fortunate because there was another Beauty of Bath tree in Gran Rugg's garden. The apples were stored on the floor of the spare bedroom and Gran would say every day, "Go and get yourself an apple, boy!" In those days we wore jerseys. The temptation was great; too great. She must have noticed the prominence, surely! Will I have to answer for that, do you think?

At Guddiford Mills, there was an orchard that contained a good supply of Tom Putts and a tree or two of Colman's Seedlings, where anyone could pick an apple; but added to lawful locations there were numerous other opportunities. And what do you say about the grass in the next field? The last pickings came from the bags of cider apples left around in stacks for Whiteways Cyder Company to collect. There were often little holes in the hessian; and little holes grew into larger holes.

Let me now turn on, to the juice.

"TAKE a bucket and go out and pick up some apples!" Gran Goff would say, and hopeful of finding Grandfather, Uncle Arthur, or Jack Salisbury already on station, I would go over the bridge of the mill leat into the orchard.

Many of the trees in the two-acre orchard bore cider apples; Somersets, Woodbines, Clusters, and many more. Usually the apples were small, and in some seasons very numerous on the branches. So there was plenty of time for the idle chatter of children as the crop was picked into buckets, to be transferred first into sacks and then into an open, wire-netting pen. In that place they mellowed, and also rotted to some extent, whilst the wasps, and the moorhens from the nearby millstream, took a persistent interest.

As the windfalls were being collected, any empty barrels that were not judged sweet enough were supplied with lime water in their bellies, before being rolled, wobbled, and swished around. That was one of my jobs. The lip of the wooden bottom platform, or dish, of the pressing device was clayed to hold water to swell shrunken planks tights, and the tub which was to collect the first oozings was soaked in the millstream. The apple crusher was cleared of any hens that had used its interior during the close season and then washed, before the great working handles were bolted on the sides.

Eventually you would find the crusher in the barn entrance, and some bundles of clean oaten straw near the press, by now complete with dish. There were several shovels, a bundle of thatching spars, and some cups, for Grandfather always made sure there was a mature brew very handy.

Then one day in autumn, when work in the fields was not considered possible, a wagon with market boards slotted in was taken across into the orchard and the pungent heap was attacked with shovels. When the wagon was full, it was reversed close to the apple-mill to complete the material line up.

Cider-making would surely be termed today a labour intensive industry, for you needed a boy to shovel and coax the apples down the hopper and between the loosely meshing cogs of the mill, and two men to turn the machine by means of the side handles. Another was needed to shovel the crushed produce to the maker of the cheese, and somebody had to keep an eye on the tub.

Grandfather Goff, occupied with wooden frame, spars, straw, and pulped apple, or muck, walked around the dish, filling the square frame set there with alternate layers of pomace and straw. Every now and then, he would tuck in overhanging straw and advance the frame up the growing cheese with spars. All the while, the new cider would be running freely into the tub, to be bucketed into a barrel which was set on timbers called jibbing, or on a special trolley.

Gradually, the apples would diminish at the expense of the growing block on the dish, and ultimately the cuboid cheese would be topped with a wooden lid. Then the twin screws would be turned down just a little to firm the top platform onto the apple-straw stack, and that would be that for a while. You could all have a drink whilst someone looked after the tub, from which youngsters always drank, in spite of warnings as to the laxative properties of new cider.

If I recall correctly, we could get almost three hogsheads out of a cheese, and this took over a ton of apples. The cheese would run well over one barrel of its own accord, and after that the squeezing began.

At first, short pieces of three-by-three oak were placed into the slots of the screws, and a couple of fellows would keep more or less time with each other as they levered each side. But later, a long, iron wish-bone tool was used to extort the juice, and I have seen three men heaving on that, going from one screw to the other.

Later, the cheese was pared around with a hay-knife and the parings placed on top of the cheese prior to a further squeeze for extra flow. In time of apple famine, the tormented cheese was pulled apart, remade and tortured again.

All the processes, leading up to a row of frothing barrels on the cellar jibbing, were fitted in alongside the demands of the corn and root harvest, and farmers were glad enough to use both young boys and old boys. Jack Wright, a blind man, helped to turn over apple-mill for years.

Although I have shovelled tons of apples through the cogs of the Guddiford apple mill, I doubt if I ever received directly related payment. Grandfather would say occasionally, "I will give you all I have in my pocket," and that invariably meant twopence.

Whether we were asked to help, put ourselves to work by handing up straw or spars, or fetched jugs of cider, we longed to be there, with the warmth of the barn, the smell of the apples, the talk of the men, and the peculiar noises of the mill. As we drank the new juice from the tub, we were next to the men, which proved that we had breached the generation gap, at least for a while.

CHAPTER 5

Local Characters

DURING THE YEARS when I walked with brother Dennis and our friends to Kentisbeare School and traipsed along the byways of the parish, cider was made on a good many farms. Now there are few presses or mills; and as the orchards have been grubbed out so has the former colour of the local characters.

As I write that, I picture a large man striding along the road, carrying a collection of broom-heads and a bundle of stems. That was Joey Orchard of the gipsy clan. His face was red and his tongue ready. I can smell, and feel, the wholesome broom-heads now.

I can also recall a tall man behind Woolworth's specs, who either came with Ricie the greengrocer, or bussed from Exeter out to the villages. On his back was slung a great brown box resembling a tea chest; and how he dragged it around never ceased to amaze me. Amazement struck again when Kirkie staggered through the doorway and opened up his device. For it possessed the properties of a magic box: on the outside dull and uninviting, on the inside cleverly designed and exciting. A flick here and a press here, and in drawers and secret compartments were revealed buttons, bows, pens, needles, elastic, laces, pencils, notepaper, collar studs, and so on. Although the Cockney pedlar's laugh and merry tales faded away twenty-odd years ago, I feel sure the wonderful box must still survive somewhere.

On three wheels progressed Charlie, the sweep. I suppose he needed that form of transport to accommodate his brushes; and bottles. Sweeping, you will realise, is dirty and thirsty work. Also, the carrying capacity of tricycles has a limit. Hence anyone booking Charlie had to lay in cider against the sweep's arrival, or the brushes were unlikely to be unbuckled. Even then you could find dealing with Charlie somewhat tricky.

Mother was all prepared one morning with the furniture removed or covered, and three pints of Whiteway's 'jungle juice' on the table. But Charlie didn't arrive on time, or reasonably after time.

"His trike is outside the Wyndham Arms," one of the shopping Tidballs told Mother.

Still she waited patiently; then less patiently, and then not patiently at all.

"Charlie is coming!" someone shouted and, sure enough, there was the sweep, looking as much red as black, pedalling his contrivance up past our gate.

"What about my chimney, Charlie?" shrieked Mother.

"B . . . your chimney, and you too!" was the retort that came out beside an upturned clay pipe; and on went the sweep; to the Four Horse Shoes, no doubt.

Mother nearly hit the roof, and when Father came home, she demanded that he should re-establish contact with the recalcitrant sweep at the earliest possible moment.

In a day or so, a quieter, conciliatory Charlie came back, did the job and drank a fresh supply of cider.

"Why is it, Charlie?" Mother asked. "Have you got to drink all the cider you do?"

"To tell 'ee the truth, missus, I've got what you would call the 'alcolic' crave!" was the drawled response.

"Well, you're the first one I have heard admit it," conceded Mother, taken aback.

The sweep had a remedy for all ills: paraffin. Grandfather Goff had a cold, and Charlie, who had called in at Guddiford Mills for the obvious reason, pressed his certain cure.

"No, I don't fancy turning my belly into a lantern," the sufferer retorted.

Raw fat bacon, small tots of paraffin, large tots of cider, and many a night with Mrs Green Field didn't seem to hammer the sweep around the ring. The tough old bachelor died at Wellington, well into his eighties. The tricycle survived in the barn at the Four Horse Shoes for some years; and I wonder if Charlie's spirit sits in the recently re-opened chimney corner where he once used to sit chewing raw fat bacon.

'Snowball' sat there, too: Snowball, who tramped an accordion around with him. He called at that same inn one night and produced an interlude of wheezing, squeezing originality. He drank umpteen pints in the inglenook, and he never 'went'. You know what I mean!

But he is gone; like all the rest. He is gone like eccentric-concentric 'Ginger' who patrolled the A373, shuffling along plurally clad in tattered overcoats. He is gone like the scissor grinders, who operated from bicycle or trolley, and who varied in skill, according to the ladies who owned the knives and sometimes sharpened them on the neck of a bottle.

Then there was the excitable Mr Sheppard who walked along bowed down between two huge cases. A lot of people were afraid not to have at least one article from him, for on refusal he used to jump and rage and curse and swear. We children used to follow him to see his antics. If there was no answer to his knock, he would thump hell out of a door, and if he was answered there was a fifty-fifty chance of a dervish dance with full sound-effects.

Other people, well-baggaged, hove to and asked, "Can you tell me the way to Blackborough Home?" which was being used as a

Church of England training centre for tramps; and when you pointed out the gaunt folly of a mansion high on the edge of Blackborough, they quailed visibly. For they had already walked three miles or more from Cullompton Station and to be shown 'Hill Difficulty' and their destination all in a moment was too much. The poor down-and-outs, often sweating profusely in summer-time, would pause a disconsolate while before re-starting the journey.

Such a procession passed: the long and the short and the tall, the cheerful and the melancholy, the open, the diffident; all on their way to Blackborough Home, where they would work in the gardens or on neighbouring farms.

One day, 'Clapp of the Moor', unshaven, in cut-off Wellingtons, walked alongside his pony and trap, singing away. Kind folk said that he was eccentric, others: "Mad!" Next day, he came by again, riding on his high Sunbeam bicycle, which was complete with gears and oil bath. Topped by a large hat, cleanly shaven, smartly jacketed, breeched, and legginged, he cut a remarkable constrasting shine. Clapp of the moor, who was a near recluse, told me in later years that he had had a motor-bike accident, after which he found himself in a lunatic asylum.

"I escaped," he said, "and everyone thought Thomas Clapp would go home. But Tom was not so daft."

He went in the opposite direction, working for one farmer for a bit before moving on to another. Eventually, he did go home, and one evening as he was coming out of the Three Tuns in Culmstock, he found a policeman holding him at either side.

"You'm too late!" said Thomas. "I've been out too long, boys. Why don't you come back and have a drink?"

Clapp moved away from Kentisbeare with his goats, to a lonely croft near Sampford Arundel, and when I was on leave from National Service in 1949 or 1950, I went to see him there. A fourteen-score barrow (castrated) pig slept in one of the rooms, and thirteen barrels of cider occupied another room. Clapp of the Moor drank the cider through the stem of a keksi, or cow parsnip.

Black-bearded Glanny Goff was a familiar figure of the thirties. He cut the verges with his scythe, made his hay by hand and then loaded it away in his second best governess car, to gain a hayrick to split between a cow and his pony. Charlie Simpson, alias Terry, kerchief and capped, pulled his handcart for miles collecting scrap, and along the way known as Dead Road travelled gipsy and mile-stone inspector.

Through the village sang the singers who said they had been scarred by wars, and sometimes a violin or bagpipe would o'er-ride the rural sounds. One came in school to play to us.

As the characters processed, another joined them: the god of war! But wait! I almost forgot Bill Harnell.

MOST of the other older men I came across were taciturn, and quite a few were downright surly. I was half afraid to speak to some of them.

"They need another pitching fork up in the hayfield," Grandfather Goff would say, and off you went, chuffed. But the tool was probably grabbed, and some remark indicating impatience flung at me: "Where th'ell 'ev'ee bin?"

"Thank you!" was almost unheard off.

It was the same when Dennis and I rushed firkins up to the fields. The miniature barrels were collared and swigged from as if the drinker was practically dying of thirst, without a word. Talk about a generation gap: it was more like a chasm.

But Mr Harnell, as Mother would insist we called him, did not conform to type. I reckon that he was lonely, living by himself in the middle of a thatched terrace in Silver Street. Father told me that his wife had drowned herself, and I never saw or heard him speak of any relations. I can picture the old fellow sitting by his neglected kitchen range, puffing his pipe. Above him on the mantelpiece were a number of tins and two discoloured china dogs. Along the side wall was a dresser and in the window was a wireless with its paraphernalia of wet battery, dry battery, aerial, and earthing leads.

Sometimes Bill would go up into the village to get his pension, but often boys like myself did his errands for him. Hence everyone had a regular right of entry, and every few days I found myself in the dusty disarray of Harnell's telling* house. Often

*A telling house, or pound — see R. D. Blackmore's *Tales from the Telling House*.

Harold Leatt, who used to cut up sticks in the back linney, was there as well, and on some occasions we would play the old man up a bit. Then he would imprison one or other of us in the coal-hole, where we peered through a crack in the plaster.

But what I especially liked was to ask the old farm labourer questions, to coax out the fund of tales he had. The telling of tales often happened on Saturday evenings when Father and I, with Dennis perhaps, went along to get the football results, which Mr Harnell would take down as they came over the wireless.

"Bring me the paper," he would say. "Show me where the fixtures be!" was the next command.

Then he would make a great fuss of trying to read the teams, as he maintained his sight was very bad. He did this, we thought, because he received some disability payment, and everyone reckoned that he could really see much better than he made out. In any event, when the voice came across with the scores, Mr Harnell would cross out all the losing teams, leaving drawn games unmarked. After that ritual, conducted in the light of a paraffin lamp, and in the company of beetles that crossed the lime-and-sand floor, the embellished experiences of Bill Harnell rumbled gently out between puffs of smoke that fractionally obscured his iron-filing whiskers.

'Baron Munchausen' Harnell could recount happenings on so many farms that one farm chap once estimated the raconteur to be at least a hundred and fifty years old. Albeit, Harnell was stooking corn one day, when his boss, who wanted to mount an assault on the rabbits as they abandoned the corn, asked, "Have you ever used a gun, Bill?" The reply was underlined by the results, when the corpses lay around thicker than the sheaves, and the barrels of the gun responsible were red hot.

Bill Harnell would break any colt, as, in addition to his know-how, a tap on a special point in the forelock brought an unco-operative youngster down like a ton of bricks. The Baron could prong eels with a specially designed fork faster than a gluttonous boy can spear chips, and what he could do in his youth with a 56lb weight dwarfed all the snatches of contemporary youth. He would hoe to a cider jar placed strategically in midfield and demolish the contents before ordinary mortals arrived. Smoking chimneys were a speciality of his. He would survey them and then make his diagnosis. In secret, lest his art be filched, he would remove or adjust a brick or so, and the chimney behaved ever after. Harnell could run, fight, work, etc., in a higher gear than his fellows, and when there was a problem, they would say "Send for Harnell!", according to Harnell. "Send for Harnell!" they said in Kentisbeare when a wagon got stuck or the binder wouldn't tie its sheaves. It remained supreme as a catchphrase when Bill Harnell, very old and arthritic, took several moments to hobble to the door.

Eventually, Mr Harnell went away to live with a relative, until his death at ninety-odd. When I read the notice in a local paper, I was reminded of the telling house in Silver Street; of a sooty kettle, money in cocoa tins in the cupboard; of a mountain of rhubarb in the garden, and the fleas that 'respectable' people said I would collect if I 'went to Harnell's'. I pictured surly old men grabbing for their cider jars. And I thought, and still think, of one rough-and-ready, friendly old countryman who welcomed one in. I smiled, and smile again as I recall the fireside hyperbole. "Send for Harnell!"...

Bill, unfortunately, was too old to go to war.

Harvesting

Blackborough House

Evacuees paddling

Harvesting at Ford Farm in the War

CHAPTER 6

The Last Lap

WHEN I REFER to the approaching war that hung like the Sword of Damocles over the latter nineteen-thirties, it may perhaps be asked, 'Could a boy of nine or ten sense the gathering storm?' I think that a child could feel very keenly that the motonous grind on the one hand of those who had work, and on the other the despair growing in the souls of men who could not find a way to earn their bread, would surely beget some change. I believe that practically everyone was anticipating the inevitable shock that would jolt a miserable train of events off its well-worn rails. I daresay that few bothered too much about the consequences.

In Kentisbeare, there were no dole queues or soup kitchens, and I know that I was unaware of the existence of such things as the latter, but there were chains of unremitting toil for thirty-odd shillings a week on the farms, or ninepence an hour with local builders. There were neither incentives, nor propitious avenues of escape. Men, I divined, longed for escape; for severance. They strained at the heavy chain of their cloying usefulness. They wanted to leave the quoin and the plough's tail; to burst out of the enclave of farm and parish and go like Kitchener's boys had gone before them, out to — they didn't bother where.

Soldiers in five or six lorries came to the village flower show one year, to demonstrate squat trucks that rolled on great fat wheels. One after another, they got stuck in a little basin of the club field. There was a lot of revving and churning, and some of the drivers seemed stuck for ever. Then one super-man went from vehicle to vehicle and coaxed and roared them out of the slough. Small boys like myself were thrilled at the expertise, and hobbledehoys identified with the shining warrior on his fire-breathing war-horse.

At that time, Father said that 'they' were building barracks somewhere; and he told me that 'Herr' was the same as our 'Mister', when I asked about the Herr Hitler who kept coming into the Daily Herald and Daily Mail. Mr Hitler was the German Chancellor, I read; and a sombre somewhat frail gentleman, Mr Chamberlain, was trying to contain the ambitions of this aggressive, flamboyant leader. An aeroplane flew back from Munich, and the black-hatted British Prime Minister walked down the gangway, seemingly excited. Somewhere, in the text beside a picture I saw in one of the dailies, I read: 'I have this piece of paper from the German Chancellor and I believe it means peace in our time.' Perhaps that is not exactly right, but in my recollections it marked a time when would-be warriors had nigh entered the lists and, disappointed, were stayed a while.

Among the other folk, it seemed there was thankfulness, expressed and unexpressed. Everyone has since learned that Britain's leaders were secretly hedging their bets against war.

Picture, if you can, coach-loads of children who spilled out and sat one afternoon around the playground of Kentisbeare Church of England School. They had come all the way from Edmonton, and as they sat there in the summer of 1939, as if up for auction, most were near to sleep, with just a few able to take some interest. The sobbing was continual.

The evacuees, all duly labelled, sat with their peculiar bundles and waited to be selected for taking away. I watched that poignant scene. I saw the children there, and the clean and spruce, the handsome and the pretty, taken off their shelves by farmers and better off folk. Less personable specimens of humanity waxed more tired and less presentable, but the billeting officers found takers for them all by the bitter end.

Neville Chamberlain and a distraught President Benes of Czechoslovakia together added up to a respite, but soon the Czechs faded out of focus and the media turned to the Danzig Corridor in Poland: war was on schedule.

What did a child think? I had a few wooden toy soldiers; guardsmen clothed in faded paint; but they grew irrelevant in the face of the reading I did. HMS Hood was an invincible battle cruiser, and on a cigarette card was the Hurricane, which could fly more than 400 miles per hour and was bristling with machine guns. I had not forgotten the shining ones in their platoon trucks. There is no doubt that I was excited as I waited for the approach, as of some grand firework display.

Then one day, a great tank sat across the front page of a daily: 'Poland is Ready!' was the headline.

An appointed Sunday came and war was declared. As I came up to the house from the adjacent field that afternoon, I found it out. Suddenly there came across me a strange mixture of feeling I cannot fully explain. But Father had joined the Territorials, and now there was a war on. The reality of armed conflict began to touch me on that beautiful September day. Perhaps I was ashamed of my secret yearning for battleships to pound each other with all their guns that I knew off pat, and for aircraft to machine-gun each other to oblivion in the huge theatre of sky. I walked alone and wondered what lay ahead.

I was quiet for some days. I watched the faces of adults and noted their hushed conversations that they assumed to be out of a child's earshot and over his head. Sometimes I — the former hawk — shuddered at the forebodings that gripped me. Then someone said, "It will be over by Christmas!"

The wishful chorus grew.

ALL THROUGH the summer holidays of 1939, we ran as usual after the rabbits in cornfields, and of course the evacuees came along to join in the fun. That posed a problem, because they had not grown up in the country as we had, and a gate or two left open, or some farmer's horses chased around, could easily harm the always delicate balance of gaffer-child relationships. Also, we natives knew that it is much the best to present a low profile, whereas the newcomers in their curiosity plied and irritated the farmers with their questions, irreverently prefixed with 'Mistah'. Gradually though, some kind of compromise was made, and as we explained country matters and showed things to the Londoners, they spun yarns about their lives in the big city.

One Eddie Turner boasted that he was in the 'black book' and in order to qualify had 'nicked' all manner of articles from shops. There was bragging about dads who were tough, had been nicked, and were in the nick, and we didn't really know whether to believe such things or not. Mother explained that the 'black book' had to do with probation, and she warned against such company. But, of course, we were literally living in each other's pockets.

When the time came for school, the natives and immigrants were integrated for a while, until most of the folk from Edmonton, according to my memory, were hived off under a teacher who had come down from the smoke with the children. Gradually, a number of the evacuees drifted back to London, which had been ominously quiet, and later we learned that some were killed in the air-raids.

And in spite of all the wishful thinking, nobody switched the war off for Christmas.

School went on as usual, and we were issued with civilian-type respirators, which lived in brown cardboard boxes between the times when Mr Painter tested them by placing a piece of cardboard against the 'snout'. There was much talk of Air Raid Precautions, and one of the cigarette manufacturers emphasised them on the cards that were always in their packets. People, mindful of the black-out and its wardens, who were on the march after nightfall, put newspaper around electric light bulbs and hoisted dark blankets across windows; and when the German bombers began to throb in their peculiar way across the night sky, all lights were extinguished. At first, any enemy aircraft was warned against by the hooter in a Cullompton factory, but later the shrieking crescendo of a siren took over.

The Local Defence Volunteers who held the stage briefly before being upgraded to Home Guards paraded around under their Senior NCO, Farmer Henry Frost of Kingsford Farm. Identified by armlet, but largely devoid of recognised military apparatus, home-spun soldiers took their shotguns along and carried through their arms drill with pick shaft and the like. Perhaps the professionals in the form of the Canadian Military Police who were billeted in the big room belonging to the Wyndham Arms, chuckled at the efforts of old warriors from the 1914-18 War, and the motley collection of youngsters who were destined to go to war later on, if they were not exempted through their toil on the land.

Father, who had been called up, came proudly home in his service uniform to demonstrate with his rifle the positions you took up before you arrived prostrate to give an invisible enemy a volley of blanks.

Still school went inexorably on, with the headmaster showing no inclination to ease up on the daily stint of arithmetic, 'Fundamental English', composition, geography, history and the like, although he had three sons in the services and, according to Mother who enquired when he collected National Savings, usually had little idea of their whereabouts. Letters, we gathered from our teacher, arrived fitfully, and I recall that weeks could go by between communications.

Sandbags, and movable trellis work well-endowed with barbed wire, appeared in the road outside the house and at other entrances to the village. Home Guards were stationed there from time to time, while men from the local company took their turn guarding the reservoir on top of the Blackdown Hills.

Each and every day, the school bell rang for the unrelenting basic stint. You will perhaps recall I had a 'girls' problem; well, I was quite used to daily canings by then, and the more vengeful I became, the more I was caned... There it was. There was no way out as long as I remained at Kentisbeare School.

"Do you think you will pass the scholarship?" Father asked me one day, and I remember I was not at all clued up on the subject.

What was the scholarship? Well, in the last year at Junior School, some children were permitted to take an examination, depending whether parents and teacher both agreed on the subject. Father, I realized, wished me to sit; but the Head resisted, insisting that I hadn't got a chance. Father persisted, and in later years he told me of an exchange with Mrs Painter.

Mrs Painter: Some people think their ducks are geese!

Victor Rugg: With faith you can remove mountains.

How the campaign was conducted after the above sally and riposte I do now know, except that a certain Saturday morning I was loaded into a green butcher's van belonging to Bill Western, and driven, I believe, by his son, Fred. Also in the vehicle were Gwen Western and Joyce Melhuish, and we set off for Cullompton Senior School, three miles away. We duly arrived, and joined a lot of children in a large room fitted out with single desks. Mary Frost, another Kentisbearite, arrived late, red, and very flustered.

Then the tests began. I did all the arithmetic easily enough, I remember, and started to eat a piece of chocolate Mother must have given me. An invigilator loomed over me, suspecting perhaps that I had some sophisticated aid. A break then came, and not used to such a vast place as Cullompton with its one main street and many shops, I arrived back to find that the authorities had been looking for me, and that a test was already in progress. I was promised by a little man I later found out was Mr Chapman, the Head of Cullompton Senior School, that I would be allowed extra time, but again I finished well ahead of schedule. There was a composition to do and I picked 'A Naughty Boy'. Reflecting on my past, that may have made all the difference.

'As a bird is to fly, so a fish is to. . .', posed the next test and I cottoned on pretty well throughout the exercise. I fancy General Knowledge was the last hurdle; and Father afterwards asked me what questions I could remember.

"They wanted to know what layers of earth were called," I returned.

"Which word did you pick out?" he asked.

"Aquiline," I said.

"Strata is the answer," he replied.

Perhaps he was disconcerted over that revelation, but I felt I had passed the test by reasoning that I had coped with most things, and therefore if I hadn't made it, who had?

I had passed. That was that: incident closed.

Weeks went by, until one afternoon Mr Painter called me up to his desk. He gave me a foolscap envelope and said something about "might be able to go." Nothing more was said, and it was only when the envelope was opened that we knew I had been selected to go to Tiverton Boys' Middle School. Strange, I thought, to have received no form of congratulations. Yet I didn't want any. I had passed on the day — for what it was worth!

I had never been to Tiverton and I hadn't any preconceived ideas about it. Grandfather said it was "behind thik 'eel!" He pointed.

Father was delighted, and much to my annoyance, praised me up and boasted of my success continually, sometimes in my presence. A month or so afterwards, he gave me a reward: one penny.

No-one else got through, and I have often wondered if one of the non-starters who were not sponsored by parent and/or teacher for various reasons, would have pushed me out of the frame had he or she been entered.

There was fierce competition between all the schools that were linked to Tiverton Middle Schools, and much was generally made of scholarship successes. Yet my achievement was not mentioned at all at Kentisbeare School! But I have long realised that I was taught by expert and dedicated teachers and beneath my childish resentment at the scholarship affair, must have lain an embryo of gratitude and pride that has grown over the years.

The days wore on and so did my clothes.

"You can't have any new gear until you go to Tiverton," Mother said. So she patched me — and thereby conferred the name 'Patchie'. It was of little consequence, for I thought continually of the kind of bicycle I should like to ride to Tiverton Junction Station; and whether I dealt out a cuff and received back the cane, I cannot say. I expect that happened.

I have a clear picture of Mr Painter struggling his up-to-date but cumbersome radiogram into school and coaxing us to listen to various classical records he had: 'The Dance of The Sugar Plum Fairy', 'The Flight of the Bumble Bee', and the voice of Elizabeth Schumann.

"I shan't bring the radiogram in again!" he used to say when the large majority grew restless.

I felt sorry for him, and I affected to listen. I watched his face for any sign as he humped his personal equipment away, and hoped he had not taken it too badly.

Treasure Island, The King's Highway, Moonfleet: they came to life through Archie.

I could not wait to go to Kentisbeare School. I was not unhappy for any length of time, whilst going there, and I felt no compelling urge to leave. I was, and am, grateful for how and what I was taught there, and tried several times to get back as Head...

I daresay my name is scratched on a stone somewhere.